Weather Encyclopedia

Peter Riley

KV-579-382

E:L RESOURCE CENTRE
KDH L15 6UZ

00000913

OXFORD
UNIVERSITY

OXFORD
UNIVERSITY PRESS

Great Clarendon Street, Oxford OX2 6DP

Oxford University Press is a department of the University of Oxford.
It furthers the University's objective of excellence in research, scholarship,
and education by publishing worldwide in

Oxford New York

Athens Auckland Bangkok Bogotá Buenos Aires Calcutta
Cape Town Chennai Dar es Salaam Delhi Florence Hong Kong Istanbul
Karachi Kuala Lumpur Madrid Melbourne Mexico City Mumbai
Nairobi Paris São Paulo Singapore Taipei Tokyo Toronto Warsaw

with associated companies in Berlin Ibadan

Oxford is a registered trade mark of Oxford University Press
in the UK and in certain other countries

Published in the United Kingdom
by Oxford University Press

Text © Peter Riley 2000

The moral rights of the author have been asserted

Database right Oxford University Press (maker)

First published 2000

All rights reserved. No part of this publication may be reproduced,
stored in a retrieval system, or transmitted, in any form or by any means,
without the prior permission in writing of Oxford University Press,
or as expressly permitted by law, or under terms agreed with the appropriate
reprographics rights organization. Enquiries concerning reproduction
outside the scope of the above should be sent to the Rights Department,
Oxford University Press, at the address above.

You must not circulate this book in any other binding or cover
and you must impose this same condition on any acquirer.

British Library Cataloguing in Publication Data

Data available

ISBN 0 19 915706 5

Available in packs
Weather Pack of Six   (one of each book)   ISBN 0 19 915711 1
Weather Class Pack   (six of each book)   ISBN 0 19 915712 X

Printed in Hong Kong

Acknowledgements

The Publisher would like to thank the following for permission
to reproduce photographs:

John Cleare: p 17 (*bottom*); Corbis: front cover and back cover; Corel: title page, contents page
(*left* and *bottom*), p 5, 7, and index page; Eye Ubiquitous/Paul Seheult: p 8 (*bottom*); Robert
Harding/G. White: p 8 (*top centre*); Robert Harding/Walter Rawlings: p 15 (*bottom*); Frank Lane
Picture Agency/Brian Cosgrove: p 8 (*top left*); Frank Lane Picture Agency/T. Wharton: p 10 (*bottom*);
Frank Lane Picture Agency/H. Hautala: p 11 (*top*); Frank Lane Picture Agency/J. C. Allen &
Son: p 13 (*right*); Frank Lane Picture Agency/L. West: p 16; Frank Lane Picture Agency/Steve
McCutcheon: p 17 (*left*); Frank Lane Picture Agency/Peter Dean: p 19 (*top*); Frank Lane Picture
Agency /William Broadhurst: p 19 (*bottom*); Frank Lane Picture Agency/D. A Robinson: p 20
(*left*); Frank Lane Picture Agency/H. Bink: p 20 (*right*); National Aeronautics and Space
Administration: p 23 (*centre*); National Geographic Society/U.S. Government Commerce: p 23
(*top*); Panos/Chris Stowars: p 13 (*bottom*); Science Photo Library/Nasa: p 4 (*bottom*); Science
Photo Library/Sam Ogden: p 8 (*top right*); Science Photo Library/David Parker: p 9 (*top left*);
Science Photo Library /David Ducros: p 9 (*top right*); Science Photo Library/Institute of
Oceanographic Sciences/NERC: p 9 (*bottom*); Science Photo Library/Pekka Parviainen: p 10 (*top*);
Science Photo Library/National Center for Atmospheric Research: p 12 (*bottom*); Telegraph
Colour Library/Pierre St. Jacques: p 11 (*bottom*).

Illustrations by Julian Baker, James Browne, Ian Heard, and Jon Jackson.

LIVERPOOL HOPE
UNIVERSITY COLLEGE
Order No./Invoice No.
L006000408
PXT8/8/06
Accession No.
526416
Class No.
372.36T OXW
WEB
OX-
RIL
Control No.
ISBN
Catal.
23 08/06

Contents

OL HOPE
UNIVERSITY
LIBRARY
PO BOX 95
LIVERPOOL L69 3GR

Atmosphere

The atmosphere is the air around the earth.

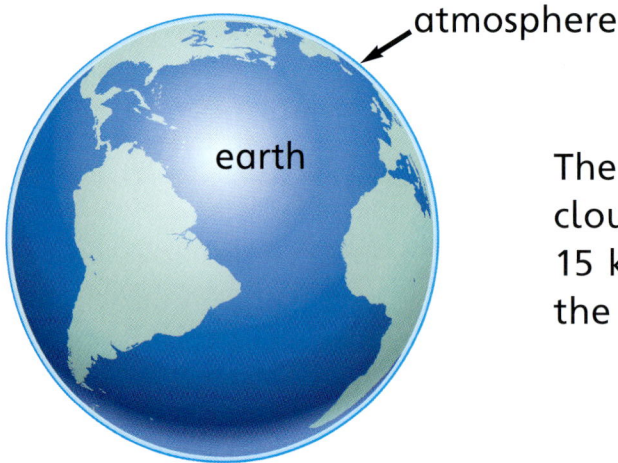

atmosphere

earth

The highest clouds are 15 km above the earth.

In a fast lift it would take about 25 minutes to reach the top of the highest cloud. It would take more than a day to reach the top of the atmosphere.

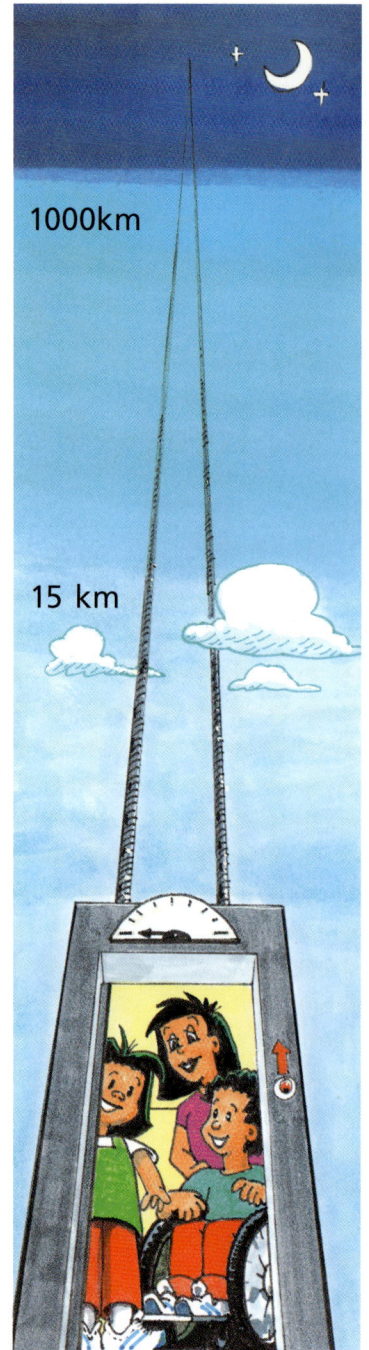

1000km

15 km

lightning

Lightning flashes in the atmosphere can be seen from space.

Clouds

Clouds are made from millions of tiny drops of water. The drops are about 1000 times smaller than this dot.

cirrus clouds

cumulus clouds

stratus clouds

Fog and mist are two kinds of cloud that form close to the ground. There are more water drops in fog than mist.

A

You can see 40 km in clear air.

B

You can see 2 km in mist.

C

You can see less than 200 m in fog.

Folklore

In the past, people have found ways to forecast the weather by looking at things around them.

The weather will be fine if a pine cone opens.

It will be wet when it shuts.

The weather will be fine when seaweed shrinks and feels dry.

It will be wet when the seaweed swells and feels damp.

When you see these clouds, rain clouds will follow them.

These clouds show you that the weather will stay fine.

In fine weather insects fly high.

Swallows fly high to catch and eat insects.

When wet weather is coming the insects fly low and so do the swallows.

Some flowers open in sunny weather and close in rainy weather.

The scarlet pimpernel does this.

LIVERPOOL HOPE UNIVERSIT

Forecast

The weather forecast is made by looking at different information about the weather.

These instruments are used to collect information about weather.

A thermometer measures air temperature.

An anemometer measures wind speed.

A barometer measures air pressure

All these instruments are used at a weather station.

There are weather stations like this all over the United Kingdom.

A weather satellite takes pictures of clouds from space. ▶

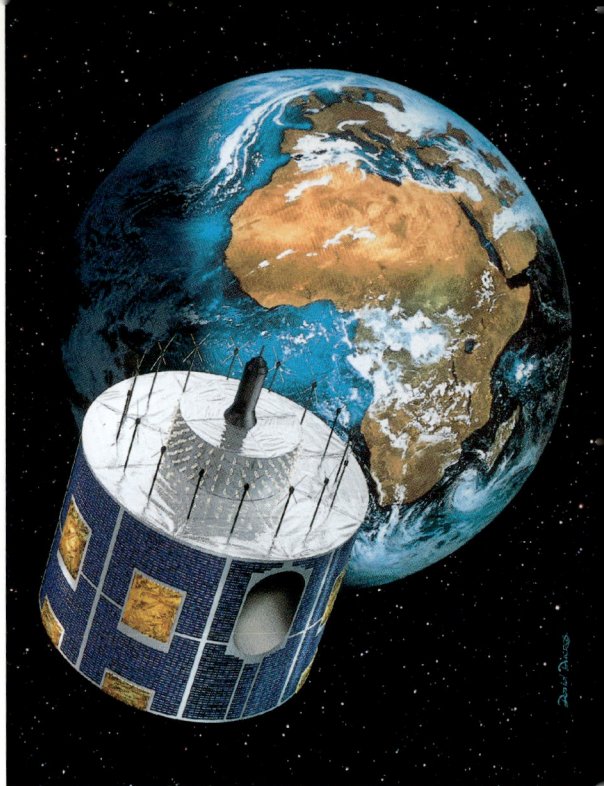

A weather balloon carries weather instruments into the air. ▼

Weather ships carry sonic buoys like this one to measure the wind and the temperature of the sea. ▶

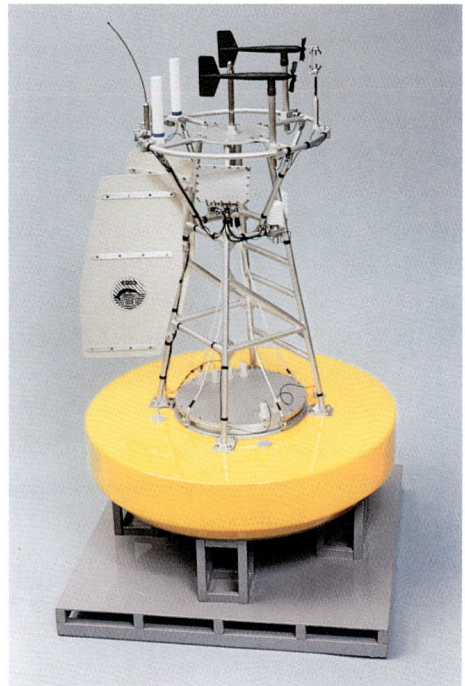

The forecaster uses all the information to predict what the weather will be like.

Frost

Frost forms when water vapour in the air cools and freezes.

Fern frost

When water vapour turns to drops of water on flat surfaces and then freezes it makes fern frost.

Fern frost on a window. ▶

Hoar frost

When water vapour freezes directly to ice crystals they form spikes where they settle. This is called hoar frost.

◀ Hoar frost makes spiky shapes.

Rime

When fog freezes the water stays as tiny drops. When the drops touch an object they make an ice coating called rime.

The rime makes the trees look white. ▶

Glazed frost

When rain falls on to a freezing surface it forms a thick coat of glazed frost.

◀ You can see icicles in this glazed frost.

LIVERPOOL HOPE UNIVERSITY

Hail

Hailstones form in storm clouds. The wind rushes up inside a storm cloud and carries ice particles to the top.

A layer of frosty ice forms on the particles and they sink down. A layer of clear ice forms on the particles at the bottom of the cloud.

Some ice particles go up and down in the cloud and form many layers of ice.

When the hailstone gets heavy it falls to the ground.

The ice layers in this hailstone have been coloured so they are easy to see.

Hailstones can be very large. They can do a lot of damage.

These crops have been damaged by hail.

The largest hailstones weigh 1kg and are the size of tennis balls.

Rain

Raindrops start off as snowflakes. The snowflakes form at the top of a cloud where it is very cold.

The snowflakes melt in the warmer air lower down inside the cloud.

The small drops of water join together to make larger raindrops.

The largest raindrops are 5 mm across

funnel

scale   water

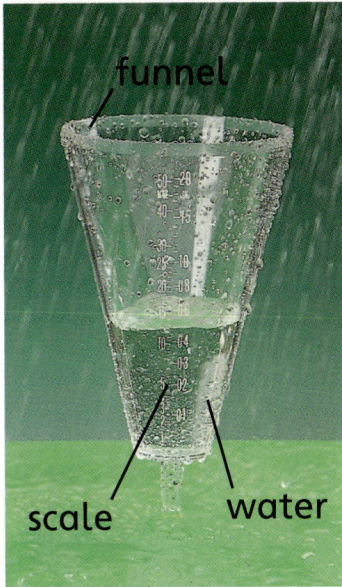

Rainfall is measured in a rain gauge. Raindrops fall down the funnel. The scale measures the level of water that collects.

15 M

10 M

5 M

1 M

The wettest place on earth is Mount Wai-ale-ali in Hawaii. Each year 15m (1500 cm) of rain falls there.

The driest place on earth is the Atacama Desert. Once, it did not rain there for nearly 400 years.

Snow

Snowflakes form from ice crystals at the tops of clouds. The ice crystals stick together to make a snowflake.

Snowflakes have six sides. The largest snowflakes are 6 cm across and are made from hundreds of crystals joined together.

Snowflakes fall to the ground if the temperature of the air is about 0°C. They make wet snow.

Wet snow is good for making snowballs. ▶

If the air temperature is below 0°C, dry powdery snow forms. The ice crystals do not join together to make flakes.

A blizzard is a type of snow storm. Powdery snow is blown about by high winds.

▲

Powdery snow is not good for making snowballs.

When a thick layer of snow forms on mountain sides it may start to slide and become an avalanche.

Heavy snowfall or a loud noise can start an avalanche. ▶

17

Sun

The surface of the sun is 58 times hotter than a boiling kettle. Some of this heat reaches the earth and warms it.

The warm earth then heats the air and makes it rise. Cooler air sinks. These movements of air make the winds.

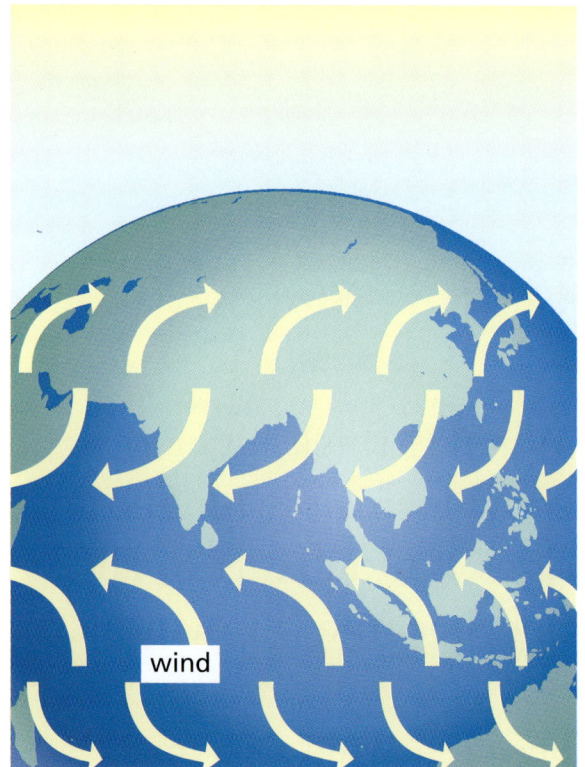

wind

The sun's light looks yellow in a sunbeam but it is made from seven different colours.

You can see the colours when the sunlight shines on to raindrops and makes a rainbow.

A rainbow is made up of red, orange, yellow, green, blue, indigo and violet.

Dust in the atmosphere scatters the blue light in sunlight. This makes the sky look blue.

When there are no clouds you can see blue sky.

Thunder and lightning

In a storm cloud, ice and dust rub together and make electricity.

When the electricity flows between different parts of the cloud it makes sheet lightning.

When electricity flows between the cloud and the ground it makes forked lightning.

Forked lightning moves at 100 km per second.

A lightning flash is 70 million times brighter than a torch.

A lightning flash heats up the air around it. This hot air rushes away and makes the sound we call thunder.

Air around the thunder is five times hotter than the surface of the sun.

You can tell how far away a thunderstorm is by counting the seconds between the flash of lightning and the thunder. A three-second gap means that the storm is about 1 kilometre away.

There are up to 300 flashes of lightning around the world every second.

Wind

When air moves it forms a wind. Some winds have names.

The Sirocco is a hot wind that blows out of the Sahara Desert.

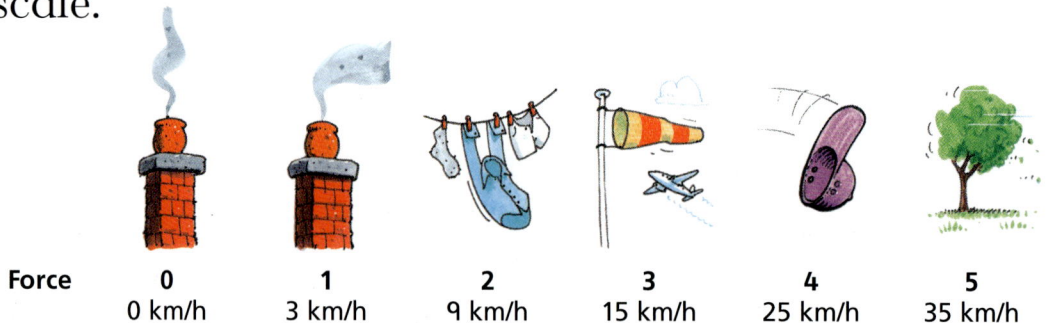

The Chinook is a warm wind that blows through parts of North America.

The Mistral is a cold wind that blows through parts of France.

You can measure the windspeed with the Beaufort wind scale.

Force	0	1	2	3	4	5
	0 km/h	3 km/h	9 km/h	15 km/h	25 km/h	35 km/h

A tornado is a windstorm. It forms over land and destroys everything in its path.

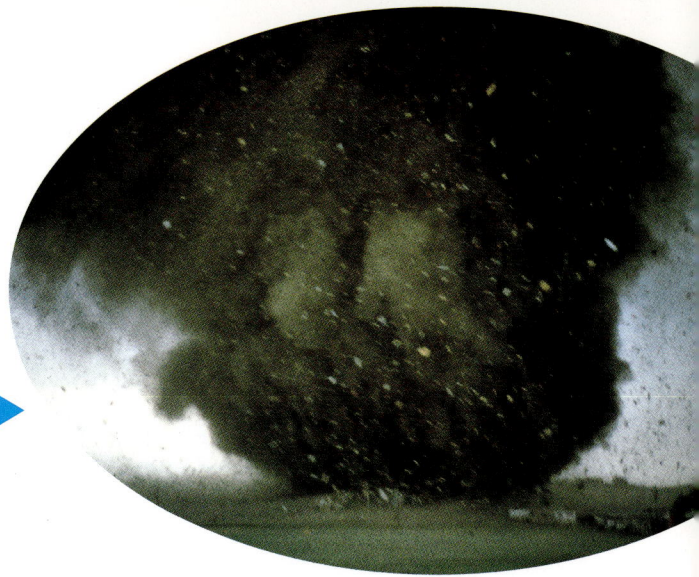

A tornado whirls round and round at up to 500 km per hour.

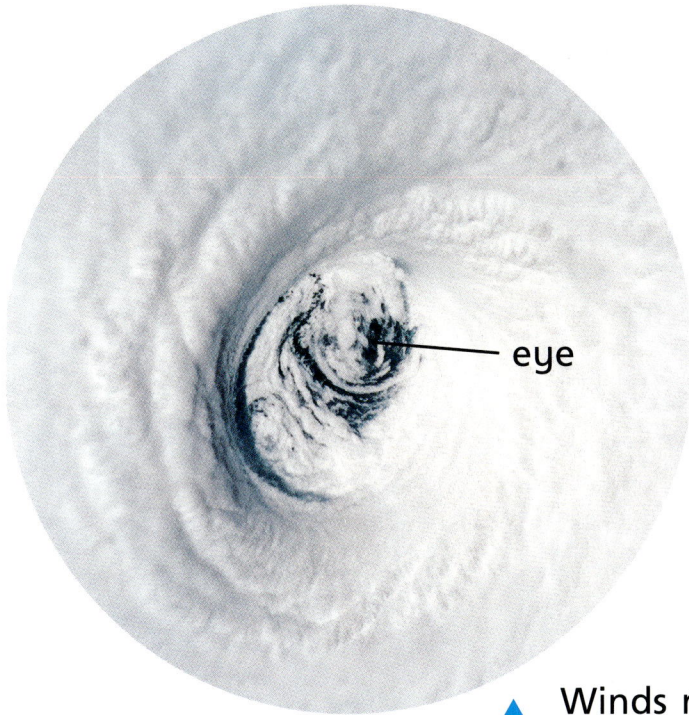

eye

A hurricane forms over warm seas. It is a huge storm up to 800 km across. The winds move round the centre called the eye. When a hurricane reaches land it causes great damage.

Winds move at 160 km an hour around the eye of a hurricane.

6	7	8	9	10	11	12
45 km/h	56 km/h	68 km/h	81 km/h	94 km/h	110 km/h	118 km/h

Index

526416

£2.99 9/2000